An Executive Trail Guide:

Thinking and Behaving for Success

Books By Terry Joseph Busch

What the Best Managers Know and Do

Effective Corporate Decision Making: Six Steps To Success

Habits That Define Poor Managers: A Rogues Gallery

Effective Organizational Leadership: The Essential Ingredients

Terry Joseph Busch

An Executive Trail Guide:

Thinking and Behaving for Success

ISBN: 9781507860748.

Dedicated to encouraging enlightened
managers and leaders.

Acknowledgment

A special thank you to my good friend Tony Starbird, whose keen insights on life and the world of management continue to expand my own intellectual horizons and whose editorial touches always manage to improve my written efforts.

Contents

Part Three

Introduction

Short of blind dumb luck, successfully traversing the obstacle course within any business or organization that leads to significant management and leadership responsibility is damn hard work. The hours are insane, the price to one's family generally unreasonable, the court politics treacherous, and you always may be one dumb move or colossal piece of bad luck from derailment. It generally takes brains, cunning, courage, stamina, and determination. Fools, as a rule, do not make it.

So it isn't unreasonable that those who succeed should be confident, sure of themselves, and certain that they will continue to succeed. Yet, so many fail, usually to their own surprise. For some it is simply the Peter Principle: they have reached their level of incompetence. Many, however, fall victim to a simple life's truth: it's what we don't know that we don't know that will often kill us.

The task of exercising significant management and leadership responsibility within a business or organization – I call it being an executive – is a conundrum: simultaneously exhilarating and exhausting; seemingly straight forward yet complex; apparently clear yet ambiguous; about being both powerful and weak; and even when safe, scary to those who are sane.

Being an executive is an uncertain risk and reward filled TRAIL to be navigated often quickly yet measuredly, boldly yet cautiously, and all at the same time. There are few certainties; perfect performance is impossible; failure is certainly an option often due to forces beyond your control; and there is always the possibility that you will be the Captain of the ship when you know what hits the fan. It is not a role fit for everyone.

Many a man and woman who have coveted being an executive have found it a mystifyingly unfulfilling experience once achieved. Some simply lack the intellect, courage, vision, flexibility, self-confidence, or stamina, needed to succeed. The executive role often becomes the very first time they have felt in over their heads.

Others are by personality mismatched to varying degrees with the realities of the job. The executive role generally demands: more attention to people than things; more focus on big ideas than on details; a broad rather than narrow time horizon; as much of one's emotional intelligence as of their sheer brain power; some comfort with not being in control; the ability to shift focus and concentration gears constantly without growing dizzy; and the capacity to sleep at night with a hundred things started yet left undone.

In many organizations, those individuals whose personalities are ideally suited to the executive role – the flexible, spontaneous, big idea, will try anything people -- are not those who automatically rise to the top. The majority of those who do rise invariably find they must adjust their thinking, work, and interpersonal styles sometimes significantly, if they are to succeed. This Executive Trail Guide is intended for both the naturals and the adjusters alike.

But who is technically an executive? This can get confusing since various businesses and organizations define this term in different ways. Only the CEO has it easy since the word appears in her title. For the sake of this Trail Guide I will try to make it simple.

If you are a first line supervisor or manager, whatever your title, you are not an executive. First line managers have no managers or supervisors reporting to them, directly oversee line activity, and require a range of substantive, technical, and interpersonal skills specific to line supervision. First line managers may find this Trail Guide of interest but less useful than the voluminous literature geared directly to their demanding and difficult supervisory challenges and skill requirements.

If, on the other hand, you have managers and supervisors that report to you, no matter the number of layers beneath you, consider yourself an executive for the purposes of this Guide. The perspectives presented here are meant to assist you in coping with the professional challenges you face. You can easily size each element of the Guide to your particular situation.

Like any Guide, this one is not a blueprint for guaranteed success. Rather it is a compendium of reality-tested insights, little secrets, and practical tips to help you along the way. Each is important, has its place in an effective executive's behavioral repertoire, and should be the subject of frequent reminding.

While I'm sure each tip can find a home in some theoretical academic compartment of the management literature, they are for me a matter of experience and the hard, often cruel lessons of real daily executive life. They are based on my years of first hand observation of executive behavior in both the public and private sectors, and years of my own personal experience as an executive who learned by getting it both right and wrong. In sum, this Trail Guide is about what works on the job.

This Guide is also about the executive behavior that generally gets positive results. By results I mean significant improvement in the bottom line, be it profits or mission success, and in the attitude and morale of employees. I mean quantifiable, measurable gains in innovation, productivity, quality, customer satisfaction, on time delivery or performance, and in whatever else you measure. It is executive behavior that establishes the norms and expectations employees are likely to follow.

This guide is divided into three sections representing one of the critical overarching challenges that confront every executive:

- **Cultivating the right mind set about the job.**

- **Developing the patterns of behavior and actions that foster yours and your organization's success.**

- **A few thoughts about summoning the courage to lead.**

I could not help thinking that he was not really wise, although he was thought wise by many, and still wiser by himself...so I left him saying to myself as I went away: Well, although I do not suppose that either of us knows anything really beautiful and good, I am better off than he is, for he knows nothing, and thinks that he knows; I neither know nor think that I know. In this latter particular, then, I seem to have slightly the advantage of him."

Socrates from Plato's "Apology"

The best executive is one who has sense enough to pick good people to do what he wants done, and self-restraint enough to keep from meddling with them while they do it.

Theodore Roosevelt

Part One

Cultivating the Right Mind Set
About the Job

The origins of many executive failures can be traced to some fundamental misconceptions about the nature of an executive's job. Clearly understanding what the job is really all about is a great place to begin the journey toward hopeful success. Although any reader may choose to differ with various points detailed below and while their organizational culture may urge them in some other direction, one ignores the following at their own risk.

Executive Performance is Not a Science

Managing and leading at the executive level has never been nor ever will be an exact science. In fact, it is not a science at all. I have always thought of it as a performing art. Seeing it in an artistic light allows one to view executive management as a profoundly human undertaking, filled with great possibilities for both extraordinary performances and a few that stink up the house no matter how accomplished we are.

Thinking of executive management as a performing art also allows us to drop any notion that the activities associated with an executive's work can be taught and mastered to the level of perpetual flawlessness. True, executive skills can be learned, practiced, refined, and honed. We can, with effort, get pretty good at what we do. But mistakes, blown opportunities, bad calls, and embarrassing moments of ignorance and stupidity will occur.

Consequently, it is how we handle our executive experiences, especially the mistakes and what we learn from them, that really counts. A successful executive must be prepared to be a perpetual student of his or her performances, critiquing their strengths and weaknesses, refining and repeating what works, and avoiding a repetition of the same mistakes.

Ask yourself, am I learning enabled or disabled? Do not just answer *enabled, of course* to this question but step back and look carefully at how you actually behave, especially under pressure. Many of the ways we react especially when things do not go exactly as we planned, represent unconscious behavior patterns long ingrained in our psychological makeup. Worse, the smarter you are, the harder real learning often appears to be.

Perhaps no one has studied and written more persuasively about the difficulties smart and successful people have with *the learning thing* than Harvard Business School professor Chris Argyris. "Put simply" he argues,

Because many professionals are almost always successful at what they do, they rarely experience failure. And because they have rarely failed, they have never learned how to learn from failure... (rather) they become defensive, screen out criticism, and put the 'blame' on anyone and everyone but themselves. In short, their ability to learn shuts down precisely at the moment they need it the most.

At the executive level, such learning disabilities can be disastrous and contagious to boot throughout an organization. The executive's challenge is often learning how to learn: to reason productively and non-defensively; to question one's own wisdom, opinion, and perspective; to consider that he just might be wrong; and to reach out for help from those better positioned to know.

Each of us must honestly judge for ourselves how we behave and what examples we actually set. Bearing in mind that you can forget seeing in others what you do not model yourself, I suggest every executive practice the following expressions publicly and often.

I was wrong.
I made a mistake.
I'm sorry.
I don't know the answer.
That didn't work, what did we learn and what do we try next.
I'm not sure what to do, what do you think.
Your idea is better than mine, let's do that instead.

These and similar expressions clearly convey an executive's openness, flexibility, maturity, and willingness to experiment and learn.

I suggest every executive laminate and mount on their desk the wisdom of American Philosopher George Santayana who warned us: *those who cannot remember the past are condemned to repeat it.*

What is it an Executive Directs, Runs, or Commands?

In Reality Almost Nothing

He'll sit here and he'll say do this, do that, and nothing will happen. Poor Ike, it won't be a bit like the Army. He'll find it very frustrating.

Harry Truman contemplating an Eisenhower Presidency in 1952.

The President still feels that when he's decided something, that ought to be the end of it...and when it bounces back undone, or done wrong, he tends to react with shocked surprise.

An Eisenhower aid commenting on Ike's first few months in office.

I sit here all day trying to persuade people to do the things they ought to have enough sense to do without having to persuade them.

Eisenhower commenting on his own early experiences as President.[1]

---

1 Richard E. Neustadt. "Presidential Power: The Politics Of Leadership". (New York: John Wiley and Sons, 1962). 9-10.

Although these quotes are over sixty years old, these personal insights into the realities of executive management remain spot on. Yet we continue to embellish our executives with sobriquets that convey precisely the opposite: Chief this or that, Director, Chairperson, Boss, etc. While our management and business publications often extol the virtues of the tough, in charge, decisive executive, the truly good ones understand the truth: patience, perseverance, passion, empathy, and people skills beat toughness and swagger any day. Testosterone is far easier to display than results.

It is tempting as the boss to occasionally engage in the *I wish it, I command it, and therefore it will happen fantasy.* Why else put up with all the grief that comes with the job if you sometimes can't just get what you want?

Well, occasionally you can but not often. Why? Because people have a frustrating, innate talent for giving you what they not you want if they are so inclined. I have talked to countless executives who told me *they will do it because I told them to or else* and then watched them get zero results. So have you. Most of us have waited out an executive or two until they quit or moved on, and then promptly undid what we never wanted in the first place. I strongly urge avoiding this dead end, career-compromising path on the executive trail.

The right mind set as an executive requires an understanding of the limits of one's power, position title, and sometimes staggering salary to move the mountain you supposedly command even an inch or two. Next, it extends to an appreciation of what it really takes to convince bright and talented human beings with minds of their own, that they should do what you want them to do.

The keys lie not in your orders, commands, policy pronouncements, or occasional displays of temper. Rather they are contained in your passion and powers of persuasion, flexibility and willingness to compromise, and in your faith that in time a majority will come to see the wisdom of your ideas.

A number of years ago, I asked my executive boss at the time what she considered the essence of her job. She replied without hesitation: *nudging things along*.

Yes, I thought, that is it, isn't it? The best executives are all **Great Nudger's**. It's about going back over and over again to ensure folks realize you were serious, meant what you said, that they understood what you said, and fully appreciate that you do not intend to relent. You learn to inch, not command, your organization forward, to get things moving and perfect them later. Although it often seems like pushing a boulder up a hill, every successful nudge forward is progress.

Admittedly, thinking of yourself as a nudger is not as glorious as being Commander-in-Chief but few executives are likely to succeed by thinking of their job as synonymous with war.

So What Exactly is an Executive's Job

The Big Picture

The best and generally the most successful executives are those with the ability to visualize the future and envision the appropriate big picture objectives for their organization. The most effective executives are those who concentrate on identifying broad, strategic goals and on ensuring the human talent, skills, resources, and motivational environment necessary to achieve them.

By the time one reaches the executive level, they should no longer be heavily involved in the daily, hands-on activities of building, designing, writing, selling, or marketing their organization's primary product. An executive's job is to insure that those who still actually do build, design, write, or sell have the means needed to do their jobs to the best of their abilities.

The compulsion to micro-manage runs strong in many of us; after all, don't we just know in our heart sometimes that we can do it better? Worse, this compulsion is actively encouraged by many organizational cultures where substantive expertise is highly valued in its senior managers.

For an executive, however, this compulsion spells deep trouble both for them and those beneath. Logically, most executives know that there are far too many things for which they are responsible to micro-manage everything. But compulsions are not logical and old habits die hard. Executives must vanquish this habit if they wish to succeed.

There are two pernicious consequences that result from an executive's determination to micro-manage. *First,* their tendency to swirl in and out of things, dipping a finger in every pie is consistently disruptive while generally accomplishing little. This swirling is distinct from a conscious, necessary, occasional strategic intervention meant to teach a lesson or impart real substantive expertise. Swirling is simply meddling out of an overwhelming need for control.

Second, nothing so dis-empowers a talented workforce as a micro-managing executive. You have too much authority to be ignored. Most likely you will receive surface compliance while generating deep underlying resentment and resistance. Worst case, the talented people you oversee will eventually vote with their feet and those who remain will under perform and resist you as much as possible.

The sort of control-surrendering delegation demanded of every successful executive requires they have a high level of trust in the ability of those around them. A few will always disappoint but empowered and trusted employees can and generally do accomplish truly wonderful things. The alternative almost always ends in failure.

A large part of every successful executive's job involves **investment**. The four primary assets every executive has to invest are their wisdom, experience, resources, and their time.

The best executives, the more senior they are, have enormous wisdom to share with their colleagues, born of their substantive and bureaucratic experience. They have the ability to broaden the knowledge and perspective of others and help them see the big picture that consumes their attention. They also generally have control over many of the resources that are essential to successful and innovative performance on the line. The best executives invest their time in sharing what they know and in making sure that organizational resources are put to the best use.

Thinking of oneself as an investor in an executive role helps one distinguish the difference between human talent and the concrete notion of a resource. I have always thought that referring to humans as resources was an unfortunate application of the concept.

Profits, contract dollars, IT infrastructure, office furniture, travel budgets, salary and bonus incentives, training, etc., are resources. Humans are those who actually do work.

It is in one's employees that an executive invests her time, knowledge, and resources the more the merrier. So act and think like an investor in the people who work for you, rather than as a director or chief, and your perspective on how to get things done fundamentally shifts.

I once heard an interview with former General Electric Company CEO Jack Welch in which he described the three principal functions of his job: (1): making the important financial decisions; (2) making the important personnel decisions; and (3) working tirelessly to insure that important learning in one part of GE spreads to the other parts. My translation: endeavouring to invest company dollars wisely; seeking to invest the right talent in the right jobs; and investing his personal time and energy to promote learning and growth throughout his organization.

How Much Time Do You Have?

How Patient Are You?

Many of the responsibilities carried by any executive can be reduced to management or administrative challenges. These can be scheduled, timed, and executed with little difficulty. A successful, smoothly operating organization tends to pretty much run itself once the requisite routine procedures are put in place and employees top to bottom are aligned with there requirements.

The rub comes when the company or organization is faltering, failing, or simply needs to head in new directions to remain competitive. Now you will be required to bring about change.

Having a vision of a new tomorrow is one thing. Having the patience, skill, and knowhow necessary to achieve that vision is something else entirely.

Disrupting the current state of things no matter how dysfunctional that state may be, means disagreement, debate, dissent, alternative visions, resistance to change, and occasional sabotage. Humans invariably resist change, even change that is ultimately in their best interest. Working through all this simply requires time and a willingness to be unpopular in some, perhaps many quarters. Patience and a tough skin are requisite requirements.

For the decisive, hard charging executive who wants everything yesterday, implementing change is among his biggest challenges. With the certainty that night will follow day you can count on this: the more wide-sweeping the change, the longer it will take. As Futurist John Naisbitt notes *things that we expect to happen always happen more slowly.*[2]

Patience and persistence are essential. Push like crazy for an unreasonable deadline and failure will almost certainly be your result. The very people you want to accept the necessity for change will likely read your unreasonable expectations as a sign that you lack the marathoner's stamina and will simply wait for you to drop.

There are countless consultants and books that can help one with the mechanics and skill requirements for implementing change. Only we, however, can produce the patience and thick skin required to see it all through. I recall Motorola's legendary CEO John Galvin once describing his company's fifteen-year effort to transform itself to an audience of enthusiastic executives.

---

2 John Naisbitt. "Mind Set". (New York: Harper Collins Publishers, 2006). Chapter 8, 63-75.

During Q & A, one executive asked how close to completion Mr. Galvin thought he was. *Oh, we're about half way there,* he replied and a sobering hush of reality fell across the entire group.

Few executives in my experience have ever seen things work out exactly as planned, or completely accomplished the bold and aggressive agenda they brought to the job. Gaining the sustaining support of an organization requires flexibility, trade-offs, and giving a little to get a little to keep momentum moving in the desired direction. Bull headed insistence on having it exactly your way will almost always generate countervailing pigheadedness in enough others to derail even the most determined effort. It is often said, *the perfect is the enemy of the good.* Not a bad executive mantra in my view.

The Importance of Balance

Any executive worth his or her salt will work hard and put in a totally unreasonable number of hours per week. But this is not what an executive is paid for. They are paid for the quality of their thinking, their judgment, their problem solving ability, and for the decisions they make that effect dozens, hundreds, perhaps thousands of people. These are weighty requirements that demand that executives be as often as possible, at their best.

Being at one's best absolutely demands some reasonable balance between work and the rest of our personal lives. Without some down time, some relaxation, some distance at regular intervals from their professional responsibilities, any executive and their employees are headed for trouble.

It is an unavoidable consequence of our human physiology that when we overwork and over stress ourselves among the first things to go are our judgment, emotional stability, and the ability to think clearly and rationally about almost anything. Maintaining our sense of perspective on what we do professionally – to say nothing of our health – demands we occasionally do something other than work.

Over the years, many an executive has challenged me on this point arguing that they see it as an unavoidable choice: either accept the workload, hours, and stress necessary to be a successful executive, or lead a more balanced life at some lower level of organizational responsibility. For me, however, maintaining a balanced life is not an either/or proposition. Rather, it is a fundamental requirement for maintaining the sound judgment and clear headed thinking you are paid for and that is required for your success.

Trust me on this point and do it. Start small; leave early one night a week. Start to experience what it is like to feel relaxed so that you will be more acutely aware when your body and mind are not.

Athletes talk about the necessary recovery time following an event. The smart executive acknowledges and accommodates the regular recovery time demanded by the stress and strain of their executive responsibilities. The smart executive refuses to wait until their performance starts to slip or worse, they get sick.

Part Two

Effective Executive Behavior

As a general rule, fulfilling the requirements of any professional job is a lot easier if we strive to keep events and ourselves in perspective. It is our work not ourselves that should be taken seriously. It also helps a great deal if we maintain our sense of humor and the ability to laugh at our own foibles and shortcomings. These traits make it easier for those around us to follow suit and vastly improve everybody's ability to perform effectively.

Who Is On Your Management Team?

The Right People if You Hope to Succeed.

Business and management author Jim Collins is well known for his advice to organizations regarding the importance of *having the right people on the bus, the wrong people off the bus, and the right people in the right seats before deciding where to go.*[3] It is hard to argue against this advice when it comes to organizational success, yet many executives for whatever reason fail at some or all of these challenges.

As an executive, your success primarily is determined by the execution of those who report to you and of those who report to them. Your dependence on them is almost total since you can never delegate or avoid ultimate responsibility for outcomes. This is the true meaning of being the boss. So having the right people in the right jobs is essential.

Don't take my word for it, note the four *master skills* identified as characterizing the very best managers by Marcus Buckingham and Curt Coffman in their still best selling book *First Break All the rules:* (1) selecting for talent; (2) defining the right outcomes; (3) focusing on strengths; and (4) finding the right fit.[4]

We all enjoy working with subordinates we like and with whom we are comfortable. But talent and job fit are far more essential. So too is having access to a diversity of view-

3 See Jim Collins. "Good to Great". (New York: Harper Business Books, 2011). Chapter 3, 41..

4 Marcus Buckingham and Curt Coffman. "First Break All The Rules". (New York: Simon & Schuster, 1999). Chapters 3--6.

points and perspectives on issues. Wise executives always have at least one or two subordinates around them with the guts to look them in the eye and tell them their idea is nuts.

In evaluating their direct reports, top performing executives begin with a hard, analytical assessment of the requirements for success in each subordinate position. What talents, skills, and experience does each job require given your goals, at this particular time? What is it you want to see accomplished by the person holding each job? Given what your boss expects of you, what must you require of your subordinates in order to deliver?

Being clear about the answers to these questions allows you to communicate equally clear performance expectations to your direct reports. They should be considered the essential requirements for a subordinate's accepting or keeping their jobs. Make these criteria non-negotiable. Compromises here usually come back to haunt you.

Next comes a subordinate-by-subordinate evaluation. How well do each of them match up skill, talent, experience, and track record wise given what you believe you must have to succeed? Engage with your subordinates, ask them tough questions about those things that matter to you. Ask them about their philosophies on leadership, employee development, risk taking, pushing back when they disagree, and appropriate business bottom lines. Their answers will tell you a lot.[5]

Pay special attention to behavioral examples from your subordinates' past work experiences that illustrate the strengths

---

5 If you get stuck for questions to ask, I suggest you read the chapter entitled "What's Next?" in Max De Pree's extraordinary book "Leadership Is An Art". (New York: Crown Business Report Edition, 2004).

and qualities you are looking for. A proven behavioral track record of demonstrated talent and performance is perhaps the best indicator you will have of probable future outcomes. Remember, *what nature left out, we can usually forget.*

None of us – executive or not -- have an inherent right to any job. We have a right to our paycheck for work done. But holding on to a job should depend upon our willingness and ability to fulfill the legitimate expectations held for our performance.

For an executive to tolerate a management team lacking the right mix of talent and skills to carry out their responsibilities, or a number of subordinates unwilling to fulfill their boss's expectations, is simply poor management.

Removing a subordinate from their job is among the least pleasant of an executive's responsibilities. Show me an executive who likes doing this and I will show you a scary person. But show me an executive who refuses to do this when necessary and I will show you the head of an under-performing organization.

It is sound management practice to maintain absolute clarity concerning measurable performance requirements and expectations with one's immediate employees. Such clarity allows for reasonably depersonalized conversations about the absence of desired results; they are either there or they are not.

While you cannot make removal a pleasant experience, you can give it an empirical basis that eventually aids acceptance. Most failing employees already know they are failing. If you have effectively matched an employee's talents, skills, and experience to job requirements from the start, the need for removal will hopefully be a rare occurrence.

The People Who Really Know Almost Never Directly Report to You.

I am completely ignorant about three-quarters of the stuff that goes on in my organization. And my senior management team, they are 98% ignorant.

Michael Gilman[6]

The people at the so-called bottom of an organization know more about what's going on than the people at the top. The people in the trenches are the ones in the best position to make critical decisions. It's up to leaders to give those people the freedom and the resources that they need.

Martin Sorrell[7]

Here are two executives who really get it. Two executives who understand that if they want to know what is really happening in their organizations, they will need to venture down into them and start poking around at the level where the organization's daily activities are actually carried out.

Unfortunately, far too many executives collude in maintaining their ignorance about what is really happening in their organizations by physically and intellectually isolating themselves. It is called Cocooning.

---

6 Michael Gilman, Senior VP of Research, at Biogen. "Fast Company", March 2000.

7 Martin Sorrell, CEO WPP Group. "Fast Company", June 2003.

Cocooning amounts to surrendering to one's *comfort zone* instincts by talking to -- and surrounding oneself with -- people with whom we feel at ease. They relax us, they usually agree with us, and when they don't discussions and arguments tend to be more fun than threatening. Motivated by a desire to remain in our inner circle, they are often inclined to convince us that everything is just fine even when it isn't.

Carried to the extreme, the cocooning process becomes an assignments process. Once having identified the comfort people, you just keep shuffling them from one position to another in your immediate circle. The potential consequences are obvious: your isolation and ongoing ignorance; few fresh or original ideas; a narrow perspective on your business or organization; a false sense of complacency; and when under attack a bunker mentality.

An executive's job need not be a prison. Do not make it one. To get the full picture, get outside your inner circle on a regular basis, venture out into your organization, and talk to those responsible for executing your core activities on a regular basis. You will learn a great deal.

Just Walking Around is Not Enough

Engage, Engage, Engage

Many executives who read somewhere about *managing by walking around*, roam their organizations, chat with lots of employees, yet learn very little. It is sort of like being at a cocktail party. You can have one delightful chat after another all at a very superficial level and come away no better informed than when you started.

The question is, do you really want to learn something and are you prepared to do the work necessary to make that happen? If yes, then here are some practical tips.

Emotionally and intellectually engage with people don't just chat. Remember, the further down the line you go, the less inclined most people will be to open up to a big boss.

You will need to gradually win trust and make it clear that you really do want to know what they think about their jobs, their part of the organization, their ideas for improvement, and your organization's future. You will need to demonstrate that you intend to weigh their views carefully and that taking a position different from yours is just fine.

Ask questions and listen carefully to their answers. Do not argue, disagree, lecture, or try to persuade them of the wisdom of your point of view. There will be other opportunities for you to do that. If you want folks to tell you things, you need to demonstrate that you will be primarily in the receiving and considering mode.

It is especially important that you strive to listen for understanding. The key to learning from others depends on one's ability to get into their shoes, to see the world from their perspective, and to understand why they feel as they do even if we do not. This simple sign of respect for someone else's point of view does wonders for encouraging the sort of honest communication you are seeking.

Above all, never, ever underestimate the insight and intuition of those who work for you. They can ferret out in an instant whether you mean to engage and hear from them or are just socializing for effect. Be sincere or don't bother.

Engagement with your employees will eventually pay special dividends when you wish to change the way something is done. Attempt to impose a change on folks who were never involved in discussions concerning their daily work lives and you will, at a minimum, significantly increase the time needed to implement the change assuming it isn't doomed from the start.

Discussions Beat Presentations Any day

At one time, I loved Power Point and all of its magical potential. But as an executive that had to wade through fifty-some slides trying to find the real issues and options, I came to loath it.

Packaged presentations are generally just that, packaged. Slick, neat, carefully thought out advertisements for just what someone wants you to know, think, and decide. You should know, chances are you mastered this art form on your way to the executive level.

In packaged presentations, points are carefully crafted, data carefully chosen or ignored, and options cleverly arrayed to lead you to one and often only one logical conclusion. My advice, avoid these types of presentations whenever possible. Consider that when you are being briefed via a package of slides, it is the presenter not you who rules the forum. You are in a reactive mode no matter how many tough questions you ask. If the presenters are sharp, they will have all the answers.

The alternative is a discussion. Discussions, even those accompanied by a few pages of data and facts, involve eye-to-eye give and take exchanges. Discussions are more spontaneous, allow for more personal interaction, are better suited to frankness, and allow you to watch your opposite for body language signals that contradict their words.

Discussions allow you to be more Socratic, asking simple questions and insisting on clear, simple, unrehearsed answers backed up by specific examples and stories. A discussion allows you to get a better feel for whether your opposite really knows what they are talking about.

Anyone can BS in a discussion but it is more difficult eyeball-to-eyeball and far more difficult to surround the message with a welter of prepackaged information. Most importantly, when you initiate the conversation, you are in charge of the forum.

There are subjects, financial data for example, and times when formal packaged presentations are necessary. But if you intend to really get to the bottom of what your employees are doing, to test their management and leadership skills, frequent face-to-face conversations about the things that matter in your organization will prove far more insightful.

According to Joseph Grenny, co-author of the New York Times bestseller *Crucial Conversations*, faced with issues where there are strong opposing opinions, high stakes, and strong emotions, a real face-to-face conversation is often essential. You have one of two choices, argues Grenny, *you either talk things out or you act them out.* Acting out disagreements in any form of passive aggression, stubborn resistance, foot dragging, or sabotage is never in your organization's best interest.[8]

---

8 From the Global Leadership Summit, August 15, 2014 and a central point in his book. These and other comments by Joseph Grenny are available on--line @ "2014 Global leadership Summit, Joseph Grenny".

The Budget and Rewards System

Use Them to Your Advantage

In a 1996 movie about a sports agent – *Jerry Maguire* – an athlete played by Cuba Gooding Jr. frequently bellows the phrase *Show me the money*. I suggest a sound executive corollary is *master the money*.

Few things define an organization's culture and priorities more than the allocation of scarce financial resources and rewards. Those who get them are de facto the *valued* and their behavior is generally repeated and emulated.

Smart and successful executives set out to get their arms firmly around the power they possess over money and rewards. Then they look for skillful ways to employ them as tools to encourage the objectives, visions, and behavioral changes they have set for their organization.

Business and management Author James Balesco argues that if you do not back your desires and your new tomorrow with money and people, they *will be combined to the shredder.*[9] In a business or organization, says Balesco:: *What gets measured gets produced. What gets rewarded gets produced again...It's so simple and so many companies don't do it. Fairness and equity seem more important than performance. Don't fall into the 'let's give everyone the same trap'. Discriminate unabashedly on the basis of performance.*[10]

---

9 James Balesco. "Teaching The Elephant To Dance". (New York: A Plume Book published by the Penguin Group, 1991). . 81.

10 Ibid.

The strategic use of rewards both financial and non-monetary, sends a clear message to everyone. If you want more collective wisdom and cooperation brought to problem solving, reward teamwork and often. If you wish to see more creativity and innovation in your organization, champion and reward it even when the results are less than spectacular. If you wish your managers to take more prudent risks to advance your objectives, reward those who take them short of disasters.

The important issue is not the salaries you pay people for their work. Rather, it is how much money various parts of your organization have to spend in carrying out the activities you wish to pursue and what sorts of behavior you intend to reward.

I have sadly watched many oblivious executives fail to get the results they want primarily because their spending and rewarding priorities continue to support something else; often something antithetical to their desires. The best executives master the money and rewards at their disposal and use them to their advantage.

Foster an Entrepreneurial Spirit

It's hard to imagine an executive who's dream job isn't the opportunity to oversee a workforce of highly talented, motivated, and entrepreneurial employees. We all grasp some version of what I call the managers magic formula: TP + HM = EP. Translated: talented people, highly motivated, equal exceptional performance.

Most executives would love a workplace filled with motivated, innovative, envelope pushers who are willing to take risks, learn from their mistakes, and keep the organization moving forward. Yet I have been inside many an organization that has no idea how to create a highly motivating working environment.

Fostering an entrepreneurial spirit is one of those concepts where intellectual intent and organizational practice often work at cross-purposes. A superior once asked me why we didn't have more creative risk takers in our organization. I recall her petulant response when I replied that she could start creating one by not always asking *who's the designated neck on this issue?*

The culture of a company or organization is formed gradually over time through its procedures, practices, and system of rewards and punishments. Organizational culture is an overwhelmingly powerful force and it can undermine even the most determined effort to create an organization that experiments, innovates, fails frequently, but always learns and grows.

Although the Dakota Tribe of old believed that when you discovered you were riding a dead horse the best strategy was to dismount, many of today's organizations opt for one or more of the following approaches:

Buy a stronger whip.
Change riders.
Say things like "this is the way we've always ridden this horse."
Benchmark other organizations to see how they ride dead horses.
Appoint a tiger team to revive the dead horse.
Create a training session to improve our riding ability.
Repeatedly insist that the horse is not really dead.
Hire contractors to ride the dead horse.
Declare, "no horse is too dead to be beaten."
Invest additional funds to increase the horse's performance.
Purchase an IT product designed to make dead horses run faster.
Declare that the horse is "better, faster, and cheaper" dead.

Revisit the performance requirements for horses.
Promote the dead horse to a supervisory position.[11]

If your organization's culture is one that encourages and rewards creativity, risk-taking, occasional random acts of weirdness, and only asks that employees learn from those things that do not work out, count yourself a lucky executive. Proceed to go, collect your $200 and try hard not to upset the apple cart.

Many executives do not work in such environments. They face cultures filled with symbols and messages of the *designated neck* and *riding a dead horse* variety. The resulting message is simple *avoid risks, mistakes and failure or else.* The resulting behavior is risk-aversion. The resulting emotion is fear.

In these situations, the most effective executives reject any notion of changing their entire organization. Rather they rise to the challenge of changing the room they are in.

These executives concentrate on encouraging and rewarding entrepreneurial behavior in those within their sphere of influence and authority. They strive to make clear to their employees that standing still amounts to stagnation, that however good their product or service may be at present it can always be improved, and that maintaining the status quo is a gift to their competitors.

Effective executives understand that there will always be resisters but there is no need to punish or humiliate them. When innovators, out of the box thinkers, continuous learners, and prudent risk takers become those who

---

11 The source is unknown for this wonderful bit of humor. I'm sure it will ring true to many of you. You can find it on line via a simple Google search. I am not near clever enough to have created it myself.

reap their rewards and advance, the message will be clear: *it is time for the rest to decided, if they are on or off the bus.*

Modeling the behavior you desire will add further integrity to your message. Innovation and risk taking guarantees that mistakes and failures will occur. Your task is to stress via your own reactions the importance of learning and future application.

Communicating your personal confidence in your employees' ability to accomplish the objectives you establish will also enhance their prospects for success. Humans have a remarkable capacity to live up to the expectations of those they admire and have chosen to follow. Your confidence in others cannot be faked. But when it is real and accompanied by your full support and assistance, it is an extremely powerful motivator.

Tell Them All You Can

The Good and the Bad

The evidence on organizational performance is quite persuasive regarding the value of keeping folks well informed about the totality of the organization's activities and wellbeing. The more people know the greater their sense of attachment, involvement, and commitment becomes. The more positive their attitude, the higher their morale and the more likely they are to feel like a trusted insider.

One very successful American retailer – Nordstrom – has institutionalized this sort of communication via a morning, pre-opening all hands session that resembles a cross between a pep rally and corporate board meeting to the accompaniment of music. Store employees are informed on a broad range of company issues including performance figures, hot departments, and star performers. I have talked to many of their employees and to a person they have told me how important, valued, and part of the company these sessions make them feel.

But it is not just the good news that must be shared. Respect for a valued and trusted workforce requires that the negatives real and potential be honestly communicated as well.

Leave aside those well-publicized cases in recent years where certain business executives lied, misled, and withheld the truth for rapacious purposes. Withholding the bad news from a workforce is often done for very noble if misguided reasons. The aim is to protect not worry or overly concern folks.

Think about this the next time you hear the phrase *for this room only.* Your workforce consists of a collection of adults that cope with life and death issues every day in their personal lives. Yet inside many organizations they are treated like children incapable of shouldering or coping with some potential difficulties.

I have had some rip roaring arguments with executive colleagues of mine over the years on this issue. Yet I remain undaunted in my belief that telling people what's up is in most cases the right thing to do for at least three reasons.

First, in many cases the workforce already knows something is amiss at least in part and any attempt to withhold information is likely to be seen as deliberate deception. Result, your authority, credibility, and trustfulness are undermined.

Second, if they only suspect something is up but lack real information, they will make things up. This is called the rumor mill and experience tells us that what they make up will invariably be negative and often far worse than the actual truth. Over time it will become their truth.

Third, by not completely leveling with people you cut yourself off from their wisdom and insights, knowledge that may be of considerable help in meeting whatever challenges you face.

J. K. Rowling author of the *Harry Potter* series, chooses to make these very same points to the young, impressionable minds of her readers at the end of book # 4. The evil Lord Voldemort has murdered a student named Cedric at the Hogwarts Academy of Wizardry. The Academy's Head Master Albus Dumbledore is under considerable pressure from his superiors to tell students a different, less ominous sort of story about events. He, however, chooses his own course. In his address to the assembled students marking the end of the school year he tells them:

The Ministry of magic does not wish me to tell you this. It is possible that some of your parents will be horrified that I have done so – either because they will not believe that Lord Voldemort has returned or because they think I should not tell you, so young as you are. It is my belief, however, that the truth is generally preferable to lies and that any attempt to pretend that Cedric died as a result of an accident, or some sort of blunder of his own, is an insult to his memory.[12]

So I repeat tell it like it is. You will be better off in the long run.

---

12 J.K. Rowling. "Harry Potter And The Goblet Of Fire". (New York: Scholastic Press, 2000).. 722

If You Say It, Mean It

If You Mean It, Repeat It Often

One of the first lessons we learn as children is to distinguish between what our parents tell us and what they actually do. This observational linking of words and actions to establish credibility quickly becomes almost instinctual as we endeavor to exploit the opportunities and avoid the risks inherent in our lives. We become skilled at testing the resolve and willingness to follow through on the part of our various authority figures. This is especially true when we want to do something that has been verbally prohibited.

Although bosses are not parents, an executive can safely assume that the same testing process is always in operation within their organization. That is why I believe dead silence on an issue or the absence of a promise or commitment, is infinitely preferable to an assertion that will never be fulfilled.

Nothing undermines your credibility and ability to lead faster than a track record of broken commitments no matter how justified they seem to you. In the extreme, an executive's unwillingness to follow through especially when the going gets tough and opposition rears its ugly head, renders one a laughable caricature of someone supposedly in charge.

One advantage of being an executive is that you can always command an audience and be reasonably assured they will listen to you at least once. Unfortunately most of us hear what we want, expect, or are inclined to hear not necessarily what was said. And just listening is a far cry from understanding.

Few things in life are more difficult than clear, un-ambiguous communication of precise meaning to an-other individual. Multiply the audience into the hun-dreds or thousands and the task becomes mind-boggling.

Being articulate and precise in language helps. But nothing helps as much as your willingness to repeat your most important messages until you are blue in the face.

Determined repetition of your message, values, vision, ex-pectations, and goals accompanied by a steadfast behavior-al consistency in their support is the quickest way I know of establishing yourself as an executive to be reckoned with. Be inconsistent or worse rarely walk your talk and you will find it hard to gather the essential ingredient of any leader: *followers*.

Do the Necessary Work to Achieve Genuine Agreement

Several years ago, I sat in a room of senior executives faced with the defining moment of a major, multi-million dol-lar reform initiative. *This is it*, said the boss, banging the ta-ble for emphasis. *We will want to move forward full speed now so I need to know are each of you on board?* One by one around the table each of the boss's senior managers issued smiles and assurances that they were indeed on board. But as we left the room I overheard one of those seniors say to an-other *we are not doing this, she will be gone in a year.* In fact, she was and the reform never reached full implementation.

Are these isolated occurrences? You know better and have per-haps engaged in a few *we are not doing this* moments of your own.

Your dilemma as an executive is that your success requires the full support and implementation skills of your direct reports and of those who may work for them. Their power to undermine your intentions is substantial and you simply can rarely command compliance.

Your direct reports have egos, self-images, their own agendas, reputations, feelings, and quirks that must be considered and navigated if their support in action -- not just words -- is to be earned. Even if your direct reports are a hand picked crew, there will rarely be full agreement on the really important matters.

Achieving genuine agreement requires a willingness on your part to listen and work through disagreements, some flexibility when you are confronted with a better argument or line of reasoning than your own, and the understanding that there is always more than one way to get to where you are going. Achieving genuine agreement requires you to behave in ways that demonstrates your respect for the holders' of another point of view.

Sadly, however, many executives act as if simply giving orders is the essence of their job, rather than gaining a real commitment to follow them. These executives are often shocked at the lack of compliance, level of resistance, resentment, and anger they experience in return. Margaret Wheatley, author of *Leadership and the New Science* describes it this way:

For me, this is a familiar image—people in the organization ready and willing to do good work, wanting to contribute their ideas, ready to take responsibility, and leaders holding them back, insisting that they wait for decisions or instructions. The result is dispirited employees and leaders wondering why no one takes responsibility or gets engaged anymore.[13]

---

13 "How Is Your Leadership Changing" © .margaretwheatley.com/articles.

Achieving genuine agreement does not mean that no decision gets made until everybody is on the same page. That laudable goal may never be possible. Participative management is not a democracy; having a say is not the same as having the final vote.

Eventually you will need to end debate and decide. That is your responsibility as the boss. Your subordinates must respect that once they have been fully heard and their views honestly weighed and considered, you must make the call.

In many organizations unfortunately, I have experienced a de facto SOP something like this: *first we decide, and then the debate begins.* To prevent this once a decision is made, the best executives make explicitly clear to their direct reports that what is now meant by *genuine agreement* is the following: *we agree that you will fully support and implement the decision or step aside so that somebody else can.*

A number of years ago, I visited GM's Saturn manufacturing plant in Springhill, Tennessee. There I discovered a rather creative solution to the *when to end the debate and move on dilemma.* They called it the *70% rule.* Debate on an issue continued until 70% of the group was in agreement. At that point the agreement became the decision. No further discussion in or out of the room was allowed and sabotage was absolutely forbidden. By all accounts, it worked.

Poise Under Pressure

You are on an airplane, 35,000 feet above the ground. Summer thunderstorms have stirred up the atmosphere and the ride has been choppy for some time. The Pilot's first *seat belts please* and *Flight Attendants please take your seats* message included the statement that this moderate turbulence would last for some time. Moderate you're thinking, it certainly seems a bit rougher than that.

Now the pilot is back on the intercom attempting to reassure that everything is under control and he states that a new altitude has been requested seeking smoother air. But there is something in his voice that suggests unease and perhaps a little nervousness and doubt. How do you feel? Concerned?

We have all been conditioned from early childhood to look to our authority figures for calm reassurance that no matter what, they are doing everything possible to handle the matter at hand. It's not that we don't expect them to occasionally be confused, uncertain, or even wrong. But we do expect that they be focused, calm, and confident that a solution will be found. I call it having poise under pressure or **PUP** for short.

I remember descriptions of fighter pilots from Tom Wolfe's book *The Right Stuff* working feverishly to pull their doomed airplane out of a death spiral right up to the moment of impact. And I recall more recently, a US Airways pilot landing his powerless Airbus A320 safely on New York's Hudson River. Now that is confidence, concentration, and *PUP*.

While executives aren't airline pilots, they certainly are designated authority figures and their subordinates and colleagues watch their moods and demeanor closely every day. This is especially true when workplace activity becomes hectic, there are problems needing immediate attention, and the general level of stress is on the rise.

Executives who become shaken easily, seem uncertain, get uptight, display anger and a temper, or seem to shrink in stature under pressure and stress do not instill confidence in those around them. No matter their actual competence, in a crunch these executives do not seem like competent leaders to those who need leading.

It is hard for any work unit to perform at their focused best when their leader does not, can not, or will not. Sometimes the results can be disastrous.

On the evening of January 13, 2012 the Italian cruise ship Costa Concordia under the command of Captain Francesco Schettino drifted off course and struck the rocks off the coast of the island of Giglio on Italy's West Coast. Despite panic among the ships 4,229 passengers and crew, evacuation procedures did not begin for almost an hour after the collision. By that time the ship was already taking on water, seriously listing to starboard, and the lifeboats on the starboard side were unusable.

Captain Schettino meanwhile had abandoned the bridge and although ordered by an Italian Port Official to return to his ship immediately, he refused to comply. The ships Second Master had also left the bridge with over 300 passengers and crew still on board. So a confused, ill-informed, disorganized and leaderless ship crew was left to evacuate frightened and panicky passengers, in the dark, on their own. That only 32 passengers died seems rather remarkable under the circumstances.[14]

It may seem unfair that an executive leader must appear confident and cool when actually that is precisely the opposite of what they are feeling inside. But we humans have come to expect that those who willingly ac-

14 See http//www.brecorder.com/top--news/109-- world--top--news/224088-- timelineofitaliancruiseshipdisaster.

cept the mantel of authority and leadership will have the inner capacity to step up to a challenge when required.

Our willingness to follow instructions, obey even seemingly unreasonable orders, and focus all of our attention and energy on accomplishing some goal, is heavily influenced by the confidence we place in the competence and self-confidence of the person in charge.

Even when we have little concrete information regarding an executive's experience and past performance record, we subconsciously intuit a mental image of it by reading their tone of voice, facial expressions, and body language. So a wise executive thinks often about how they come across under stress or in a crisis. If uncertain, they ask some colleagues for a *no-kidding* assessment. The more self-awareness an executive develops, the more self-control they gain.

The best executives never confuse letting others know they want their help to figure out a correct course of action, with displaying a lack of self- confidence. Rather it is a mature way of indicating your confidence that a collective set of inputs will likely develop a better set of options than relying on your instincts alone. What others care about is your focused and confident ability to develop possible solutions, not on you having them all yourself.

The Talent You Leave behind Really Matters

With exceptions generally at the top, most rising executives can anticipate an average of three to five years on any given job. This is not an exceptional amount of time to accomplish big changes and goals. The resisters, who generally measure their tenure in much longer time frames, are often just waiting you out. Thus your legacy will largely depend on the talent and commitment to your goals you leave behind.

I call it *seeding your organization with the right people, in the right positions, to keep momentum moving long after you depart.* This is not simply a matter of identifying and assigning talent. To a much larger degree, it is about your personal mentoring, coaching, employee development, and leadership skills. It is about the gradual development of a sustaining, passionate commitment to your long-range vision among enough others so your departure does not mean a quick reversal of direction.

This is another time consuming, people-oriented, requirement of a successful executive's job. But by now I'm sure you have figured out that a successful executive will end up spending close to 80% of her time on these *people issues* in one form or another. Your legacy of sustainable accomplishments is but another challenge that depends upon it.

Part Three

Having the Courage to Lead

Throughout this Guide I have used the terms manage and lead liberally. Good executives will, over time, do plenty of both. Now it is time to distinguish between the two terms in order to clarify the difference and highlight the requirements, challenges, and risks involved in making the decision to lead.

Ronald Heifitz, co-founder of the Center for Public Leadership at the Harvard Kennedy School, defines the act of leadership as *getting people to do adaptive work.*

When the task at hand is one with a tried and true approach to its solution and there is broad agreement on who needs to do what, argues Helfitz, no adaptive work is required. Somebody with management and organizing skills may be needed to synchronize the activities of others but there will be general agreement on what and how things should proceed.

But what happens when, despite unanimous agreement that a problem exists, there is no agreement on how precisely to tackle it? What happens when some may believe nothing should be done at all? Convincing others that a new direction or change is necessary will require somebody to step up to the leadership challenge of getting humans to engage in some form of adaptive work.[15]

Michael Useem devotes a chapter in his book *The Leadership Moment* to Clifton R. Wharton Jr. In 1987, at the age of 60, Wharton was successfully running New York's Public University system and nearing retirement. Yet he agreed to take on the monumental challenge of restructuring *a major institution from top to bottom and bring a great company into the twentieth century;*[16] specifically the Teachers Insurance and Annuities Association- College Retirement Equities Fund or TIAA/CREF. It was an organization seriously out of touch with its customers and its markets. Despite all the obstacles, doubters, and critics, when Wharton left TIAA-CREF in 1993 it had been modern-

---

15 Ronald A Heifitz, Leadership Without Easy Answers. (Boston: Harvard University Press, 1994), Chapter 3.

16 Michael Useem. "The Leadership Moment". (New York: Random House, 1998). 155

ized, its monopoly over most teachers' retirement options had ended, and investment choices were opened to the membership.[17]

In his book *The Tipping Point*, Malcolm Gladwell describes how a TV producer named Joan Ganz Cooney set out to *create a learning epidemic to counter the prevailing epidemics of poverty and illiteracy among children from disadvantaged homes.*[18] Her concept was called **Sesame Street.** The idea challenged the very heart of conventional educational wisdom at the time, which believed that good teaching had to be interactive and respond to children individually. Television, the educators argued, was a passive, low involvement, mass audience talking box. Ms. Cooney was to prove her critics wrong.[19]

In the early 1990s, General Motors' executives personally informed 3,500 stunned car builders at its Wilmington Delaware assembly plant that the plant would close in 1996 to reduce costs. There was nothing they could do to effect this decision the GM executives told the shocked employees. When the executives departed, plant manager Ralph Harding made an impassioned speech to the entire workforce boldly proclaiming that while there may be nothing they could do to change GM's mind, they could make them *look really stupid* because they are going to be closing the best plant in General Moters.[20] Over the next three years, Harding galvanized his workforce and successfully transformed the Wilmington plant into a model for the entire GM system. In 1996, the plant remained open.

---

17 Ibid., Chapter 6. 18

18 Malcolm Gladwell."The Tipping Point". (Boston: Little Brown and Company, 2000). 89.

19 Ibid., Chapter 3.

20   "Fast Company". August 2003. . 65.

What did each of these visionary executives have in common? Each was prepared to exert active leadership whatever the odds and eventual outcome, with little more than their self-confident, passionate belief that their course of action was right.

Joel Barker in his book *Paradigms: the Business of Discovering the Future* discusses the difference between managing and leading by likening the act of leading adaptive work to a paradigm shift:

Managers manage within a paradigm. What allows you to manage within a paradigm are the rules, the guiding principles, the system, the standards, the protocols. Give a good manager the system, and the manager will optimize it.[21]

You lead, contends Barker, between paradigms and:

New paradigms put everyone practicing the old paradigm at great risk. The higher one's position, the greater the risk. The better you are at the old paradigm, the more you have invested in it, the more you have to lose by changing paradigms.[22]

Defined in these terms, it is easy to see why leadership is hard, often dangerous, and not for the faint of heart. You must be willing to take risks and to face the ire of those who wish you to keep it simple, predictable, the way it's always been, and above all safe.

Only time will tell if you are right and yet, despite all the uncertainties, you must convince others to follow you. Clifton Wharton, Joan Cooney and Ralph Harding were essentially asking people to have faith that working together with them, the best course of action for everyone could be found.

---

21 Joel Arthur Barker. "Paradigms: The Business of Discovering The Future". New York: Harper Collins Publishers, 1992. P. 164
22 Ibid., 69.

So leadership is every bit as much about what is in your heart as it is about your IQ. Daniel Goleman, author of the best selling book *Emotional Intelligence*, puts it this way: *IQ and technical skills are important but I have found that the most effective leaders are alike in one crucial way: they all have a high degree of what has come to be known as emotional intelligence.* [23] Specifically:

Self-awareness
Emotional self-regulation
Motivation to achieve
Empathy for others
The social skill to manage and maintain relationships.[24]

In the end, leadership is about having courage and guts. You cannot lead without risk, danger, the possibility of failure, and the reality that in the end you may have taken a lot of other folks down the wrong road.

This is a pretty awesome responsibility to assume and for which you will be held accountable. If this does not scare you a little, perhaps you are confused about the task ahead. If it does raise just a few hairs on the back of your neck, then at least you are thinking clearly about what might lie ahead. In the end you will need to face your fears and find the courage to *just do it anyway.*

---

23 Daniel Goleman. "What Makes A Leader"? *Harvard Business Review.* November--December 1998. P. 94.

24 Ibid, 95-102

Final Thoughts

This Trail Guide's overarching message is that your chances of performing effectively at the executive level can be greatly enhanced by: maintaining the right perspective on executing the responsibilities entrusted to you; by cultivating a set of daily behaviors designed to unleash and motivate the talent at your disposal; and by knowing when it is time to lead, not manage risks and all.

I will assume at this point that you have fully digested the contents of this Guide and have begun the process of internalization and emulation. So to avoid summing up by repeating what you have just read I offer the following executive caricatures. It is my hope that the tips contained in this Guide will help you avoids becoming one of these.

The Tyrant – a rigid, authoritarian, impatient, micro-managing, control freak. They yell a lot, prefer to give orders rather than persuade, want everything done now and exactly their way, think compromise is for sissies, and believe folks will do it because the boss said so.

The-Know-it-all – brain smart but not very wise. They stopped learning years ago, ignore the lessons of their mistakes, would rather broadcast than listen, and are unshakably convinced that they are smarter and better than everyone else in the room.

The Hermit King – prisoners in their own castle. They are surrounded by their sycophantic courts and remain mostly ignorant of their Kingdom's well being.

The Politician – let others take the risks. They believe information is power so they share it grudgingly, reward loyalty before talent, will trade follow-through and consistency for popularity, and will always seek someone else to blame.

The-heart-attack-waiting-to-happen – the work- a-holic who believes BALANCE is a type of scale not a life choice.

If you unfortunately see yourself in any or a combination of the above, I suggest a re-reading of this guide is in order.

Finally, a word to the wise. When confronted by the enemy of every executive, someone who believes your approach to executive performance is absolutely wrong, remember Murphy's First Law of Debate: *never argue with a fool – people might not know the difference.*

About the Author

Terry Joseph Busch, Ph. D has over forty years of broad professional experience as a teacher, international affairs analyst, manager, senior executive, consultant, and public speaker. His early work experience included stints as an Army Medical Services Corps Officer in Germany and Vietnam, and an Assistant Professorship in the Political Science Department at Denison University in Ohio. His distinguished career with the Central Intelligence Agency included senior assignments as Director of Leadership Analysis in the Directorate of Intelligence, Deputy Inspector General, and Director Human Resource Management. He is now President and CEO of his own management consulting practice.